Say "Thank you" when . . .

your friend gives you half her
apple . . .

your brother helps you weed the garden . . .

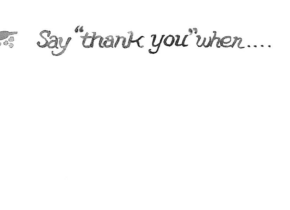

your mother gives you a
compliment . . .

a friend gives you a birthday present . . .

Say "thank you" when....

your brother finds your missing shoe . . .

Grandma makes your favorite
dinner . . .

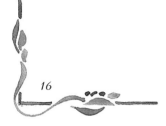

Say "thank you" when....

your dad plays ball with you . . .

your mom bandages your knee . . .

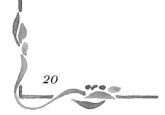

Say "thank you" when....

someone picks up a crayon you dropped . . .

your teacher helps you solve a problem . . .

someone opens a door for you . . .

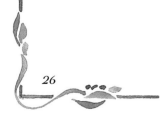

a friend helps you carry your books . . .

Grandpa takes you to the zoo.

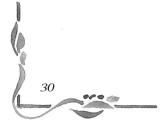

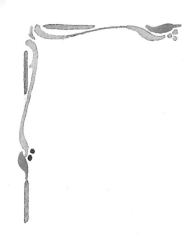

Say "Thank you" to show appreciation
for what someone has done.

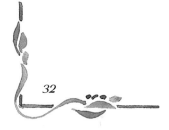